inside
PLANTS

First published in 2011 by Miles Kelly Publishing Ltd
Harding's Barn, Bardfield End Green, Thaxted, Essex, CM6 3PX, UK

Copyright © Miles Kelly Publishing Ltd 2011

This edition printed in 2012

10 9 8 7 6 5 4 3 2 1

Publishing Director: Belinda Gallagher
Creative Director: Jo Cowan
Design Concept: Simon Lee
Volume Design: Rocket Design
Cover Designers: Kayleigh Allen, Simon Lee
Indexer: Gill Lee
Production Manager: Elizabeth Collins
Reprographics: Stephan Davis, Jennifer Hunt,
Thom Allaway
Consultant: Camilla de la Bedoyere
Edition Editor: Amanda Askew

ISBN 978-1-84810-841-7

Printed in China

British Library Cataloguing-in-Publication Data
A catalogue record for this book is available from the British Library

Every effort has been made to acknowledge the source and copyright
holder of each picture. Miles Kelly Publishing apologises for any
unintentional errors or omissions.

MADE WITH PAPER FROM

A SUSTAINABLE FOREST

inside
PLANTS

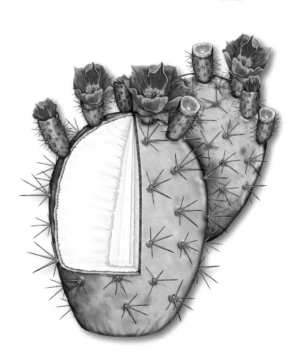

By Steve Parker
Illustrated by Peter Bull Art Studio

Miles
Kelly

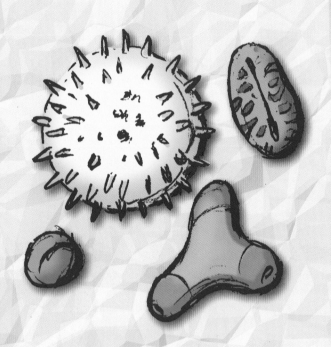

ACKNOWLEDGEMENTS

All panel artworks by Rocket Design

The publishers would like to thank the following sources for the use of their photographs:

Back cover: Shutterstock: Denise Kappa

Fotolia: 16 Robert Ford; 25 Jefery

Shutterstock: COVER Tungphoto, Cathy Keifer; 6(t) tonyz20, (b) B.G. Smith, (c) Anton Foltin; 7(t) Dr. Morley Read; 8 mlorenz; 10 Shi Yali; 12 Kang Khoon Seang; 15 Denise Kappa; 18 Daniel Hebert; 20 Robert Hardholt; 22 Cathy Keifer; 26 Heather A. Craig; 29 Dr. Morley Read; 30 AJP; 32 Brykaylo Yuriy; 35 Nazzu; 36 szefei

All other photographs are from Miles Kelly Archives

WWW.FACTSFORPROJECTS.COM

Each top right-hand page directs you to the Internet to help you find out more. You can log on to **www.factsforprojects.com** to find free pictures, additional information, videos, fun activities and further web links. These are for your own personal use and should not be copied or distributed for any commercial or profit-related purpose.

If you do decide to use the Internet with your book, here's a list of what you'll need:

• A PC with Microsoft® Windows® XP or later versions, or a Macintosh with OS X or later, and 512Mb RAM

• A browser such as Microsoft® Internet Explorer 9, Firefox 4.X or Safari 5.X
• Connection to the Internet. Broadband connection recommended
• An account with an Internet Service Provider (ISP)
• A sound card for listening to sound files

Links won't work?
www.factsforprojects.com is regularly checked to make sure the links provide you with lots of information. Sometimes you may receive a message saying that a site is unavailable. If this happens, just try again later.

Stay safe!
When using the Internet, make sure you follow these guidelines:
• Ask a parent's or a guardian's permission before you log on.
• Never give out your personal details, such as your name, address or email.
• If a site asks you to log in or register by typing your name or email address, speak to your parent or guardian first.
• If you do receive an email from someone you don't know, tell an adult and do not reply to the message.
• Never arrange to meet anyone you have talked to on the Internet.

Miles Kelly Publishing is not responsible for the accuracy or suitability of the information on any website other than its own. We recommend that children are supervised while on the Internet and that they do not use Internet chat rooms.

www.mileskelly.net

info@mileskelly.net

CONTENTS

INTRODUCTION. 6

PARTS OF A PLANT 8

ROOTS AND STEMS 10

LEAVES 12

FLOWERS. 14

POLLINATION 16

GERMINATION 18

PLANT DEFENCES. 20

CARNIVOROUS PLANTS 22

PARASITIC PLANTS 24

SEAWEEDS. 26

MOSS. 28

FERNS 30

CONIFERS. 32

BROADLEAVED PLANTS 34

RAINFORESTS 36

GLOSSARY 38

INDEX. 40

INTRODUCTION

In order to survive and grow successfully, plants need certain conditions. They require sunlight, temperatures above freezing, and at least some moisture. Luckily for animals, which depend on plants for food and oxygen, these conditions exist almost worldwide. For land plants, warmer and wetter habitats are usually preferable. However, some watery habitats, such as swamps, are low in the carbon dioxide and oxygen gases that plants also need to survive.

The Florida Everglades in the US enjoy year-round sunshine, warmth and water – it's a plant paradise.

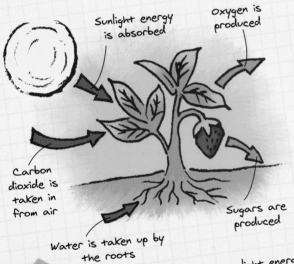

Sunlight energy is absorbed

Oxygen is produced

Carbon dioxide is taken in from air

Water is taken up by the roots

Sugars are produced

Plants use sunlight energy to live, grow and make fruits.

LIGHT WORK

Photosynthesis is the process used by many plants to make their own foods. Leaves trap light energy from the Sun, then use it to combine carbon dioxide from the air and water from the soil to form sugars. The energy and nutrients are especially concentrated in seeds and their fruits, which is why many animals forage for them. Plants use most of their high-energy foods to build new parts and tissues from minerals and nutrients absorbed from soil. Importantly, during photosynthesis oxygen is given off. It is vital for both plants and animals to take in oxygen in order to survive.

Even when plants stop growing in winter, they are food for hungry animals such as deer

The topics featured in this book are Internet linked.
Visit www.factsforprojects.com to find out more.

Rather than making their own stems, rainforest orchids grow on trees.

LOVE HUMIDITY

All plants, no matter how well adapted to deserts and drought, slowly lose moisture. They give off water vapour from their inner tissues into the air. Dry air and winds encourage even more water loss. The reverse happens in humid tropical rainforests due to the moist air and still conditions. Without the need to conserve water, rainforest plants can grow succulent stems, bursting buds, luscious leaves, fabulous flowers and juicy fruits. The main limit for plants in this climate type is light, so crowds of plants grow upwards towards the sky, trying to reach every available ray of sunshine.

There are almost half a million different kinds, or species, of plants.

Large saguaro cacti are the 'trees' of their dry scrub and desert habitats.

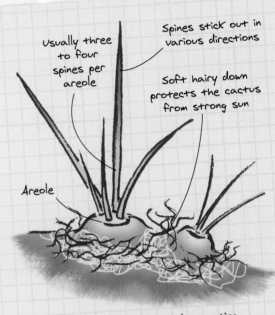

Usually three to four spines per areole

Spines stick out in various directions

Soft hairy down protects the cactus from strong sun

Areole

Cacti fend off herbivores (plant-eating animals) with spines, and are protected against the Sun and wind by hairy down.

ENDLESS STRUGGLE

As well as coping with extreme conditions and soils lacking in nutrients, plants also have to defend themselves against plant eaters. Cacti, acacias and brambles have sharp spines or thorns to put off herbivores. Some plants have leaves that contain substances called tannins, making them too tough to chew, while others have a horrible taste. There are even deadly poisonous berries.

PARTS OF A PLANT

Some plants are little more than tiny, simple collections of microscopic cells. Others are much more complex organisms, with many different parts. The most complex are flowering plants such as herbs, flowers, grasses, bushes and trees. Flowering plants have four main sets of parts: roots in the ground, a stem to hold the plant up, leaves to gather the Sun's light energy, and flowers to reproduce.

Did you know?

The first plants were tiny specks of green jelly floating in the oceans more than 2500 million years ago. Larger seaweed-type plants lived around 1000 million years ago. The first small plants began to grow on land from around 500 million years ago.

✳ LIFE support

Plants are 'primary producers'. They capture light energy and convert it into sugars and other high-energy substances. Herbivorous animals cannot do this. They are 'primary consumers' and get their energy by consuming plants. So plants are the basis of most food chains on Earth, but not all. Some animals survive on energy contained in mineral substances found in hot water spurting out of the deep seabed. Here it is so dark that no plants grow. The energy is captured by 'friendly' microbes in the animals' bodies.

Flowers Bright, showy flower petals attract animals to carry a plant's pollen to other flowers of its kind. Usually all the flowers on one plant bloom at the same time, when it is warm and sunny and animals are active.

When a flower opens out from inside its bud, it can increase its volume more than 100 times — mainly by its cells taking in water.

Soil surface

Leaves The wide, flat yet thin leaf is the best shape for absorbing light energy and exchanging gases with the surrounding air. Each leaf has an attachment stalk called a petiole.

The biggest land animals, such as moose, are entirely vegetarian

Roots The growing root tips lengthen and push their way between soil particles. The older, thicker parts have strong fibres.

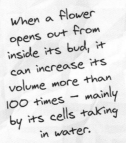

Watch a video to find out why plants are so important by visiting www.factsforprojects.com and clicking on the web link.

Golgi body

Central vacuole

Chloroplast

Endoplasmic reticulum

Cell wall

Nucleus

Buds Flowers develop many weeks before they unfurl, inside small buds. The delicate inner parts are enlosed and protected by an outer greenish casing of tougher curved parts known as sepals.

Secondary stem

The strange welwitschia plant of southern African deserts has just two permanent leaves, which may be over 500 years old.

Petiole

Main stem This is the stiffest part of the plant. It is strengthened by long, tough fibres inside, to carry the weight of the above-ground parts and resist snapping in wind.

✳ How do PLANT CELLS work?

Plant cells are so small that 100 would fit in this 'o'. The strong, stiff outer wall gives the whole cell its shape. Within this is cytoplasm, a liquid in which dozens of tiny parts float. These include folded sheets of membranes called endoplasmic reticulum, where new parts for the cell are made, and golgi bodies, where substances such as sap (a fluid that transports water and nutrients) are made that will be exported from the cell. Chloroplasts turn sunlight energy into sugars and similar products. At the centre of the cell is a vacuole that contains stores of minerals and water, as well as temporary wastes.

The roots of some desert trees spread out more than 100 m through the dry soil in their search for precious moisture.

Roots absorb nutrients

ROOTS AND STEMS

Roots anchor a plant into the ground, and also take in water and simple mineral substances from the soil. Tiny tubes in the stem carry water and minerals up to the higher parts of the plant. Stems also hold these parts above the ground, away from small herbivorous animals, nearer to sunlight, and above other plants nearby competing for light.

Did you know?

Wood is inedible to humans but it is consumed by many animals, from termites to grubs, deer, elephants, and even a newly discovered, 70-cm-long catfish in the Amazon River. Microbes in the guts of these animals break down the tough fibres.

The tallest 'stems' are the trunks of the highest trees, strengthened with woody fibres called lignin.

Cortex of large cells

Epidermis and cuticle

A group of aspen trees all grow from one seedling and share one giant root system that may be tens of kilometres across.

Bamboo is one of the fastest growing plants

Outer stem Around the main xylem and phloem is the cortex, a thicker layer of large cells that helps to stiffen the main stem and store nourishment. The epidermis is the stem's outermost 'skin', and is covered by a waxy, waterproof layer known as the cuticle.

✳ SUPER shoots

In regions with cold winters and hot summers, the warmth and lengthening daylight of spring sees a burst of plant growth. Stems grow fast to get above their rivals and make sure their leaves and flowers are in the best place to open. In tropical areas, the same happens when the rainy season follows the dry. Fastest growing is bamboo, a grass with tree-like strengthening woody fibres in its stems. In good conditions it can lengthen by 40 centimetres in one day, with the record-holder at almost 100 centimetres in a day.

Smaller roots As the root tips push through the soil, the remaining roots gradually thicken and strengthen to provide ever-increasing anchorage, as the plant grows above ground.

Find out interesting facts about the different kinds of plant roots by visiting www.factsforprojects.com and clicking on the web link.

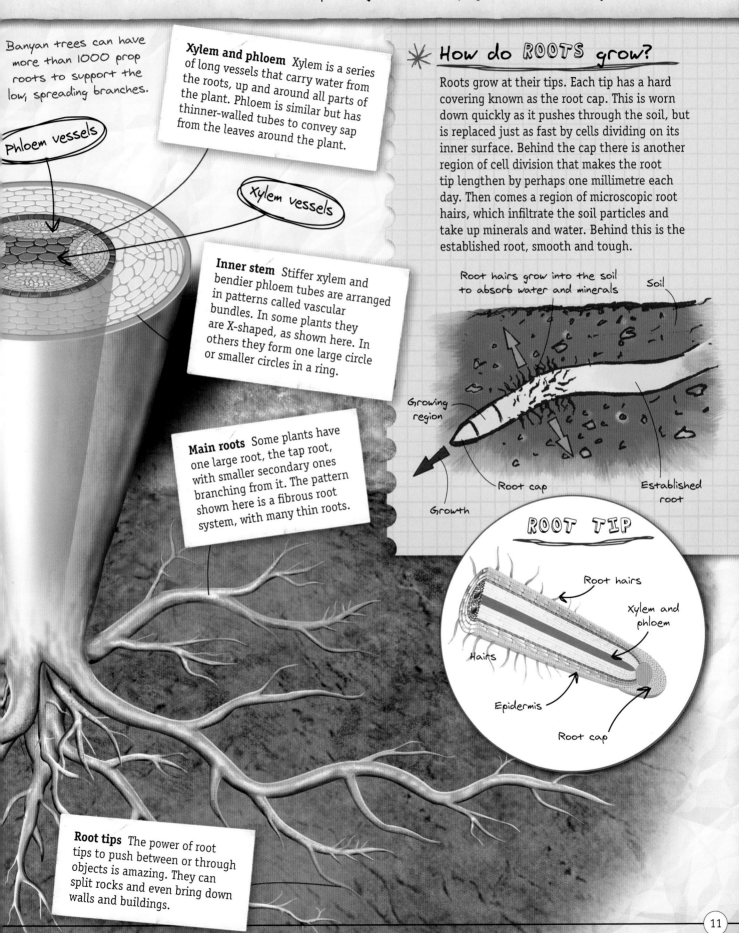

Banyan trees can have more than 1000 prop roots to support the low, spreading branches.

Phloem vessels

Xylem and phloem Xylem is a series of long vessels that carry water from the roots, up and around all parts of the plant. Phloem is similar but has thinner-walled tubes to convey sap from the leaves around the plant.

Xylem vessels

Inner stem Stiffer xylem and bendier phloem tubes are arranged in patterns called vascular bundles. In some plants they are X-shaped, as shown here. In others they form one large circle or smaller circles in a ring.

Main roots Some plants have one large root, the tap root, with smaller secondary ones branching from it. The pattern shown here is a fibrous root system, with many thin roots.

Root tips The power of root tips to push between or through objects is amazing. They can split rocks and even bring down walls and buildings.

✳ How do ROOTS grow?

Roots grow at their tips. Each tip has a hard covering known as the root cap. This is worn down quickly as it pushes through the soil, but is replaced just as fast by cells dividing on its inner surface. Behind the cap there is another region of cell division that makes the root tip lengthen by perhaps one millimetre each day. Then comes a region of microscopic root hairs, which infiltrate the soil particles and take up minerals and water. Behind this is the established root, smooth and tough.

Root hairs grow into the soil to absorb water and minerals

Soil

Growing region

Root cap

Growth

Established root

ROOT TIP

Root hairs

Xylem and phloem

Hairs

Epidermis

Root cap

LEAVES

Leaves are living solar panels. Their task is to take in or trap light energy and convert it into chemical energy, usually in the form of sugars dissolved in water, which make sweet-tasting sap. Some of the tiny tubes in a leaf bring water as a raw material needed to make sap. Other tubes take the sap away to be distributed all around the plant as an energy source.

Did you know?

Most leaves are green because they contain the light-catching green pigment, or coloured substance, called chlorophyll. But some leaves are different colours because they have other photosynthetic pigments – orange carotene, yellow xanthophyll or brown phaeophytin.

The spectacular floating leaves of the giant waterlily

✳ GREEN carpets

Most leaves are broad and thin, like sheets. This shape gives a large surface area for absorbing light, and also allows the carbon dioxide needed for photosynthesis to reach the inner parts easily. As well as capturing light, leaves are specialized for various conditions. Waterlily leaves have a thick, waxy covering or cuticle so they float rather than becoming waterlogged. The giant waterlily leaf even has an upturned rim to prevent water flowing over it and making it sink.

Layers The outer cell layers are the epidermis. Below the upper epidermis are elongated cells packed together, the palisade layer. Beneath is the open, irregular spongy layer.

Chloroplasts These convert energy from sunlight into sugars. Most chloroplasts are in the long, upright cells of the palisade layer. They are just under the epidermis and so receive the most light.

Vascular bundles (veins) Like blood vessels in the body, narrow bundles of phloem and xylem branch to all parts of the leaf. Larger ones form noticeable thickenings or 'veins'.

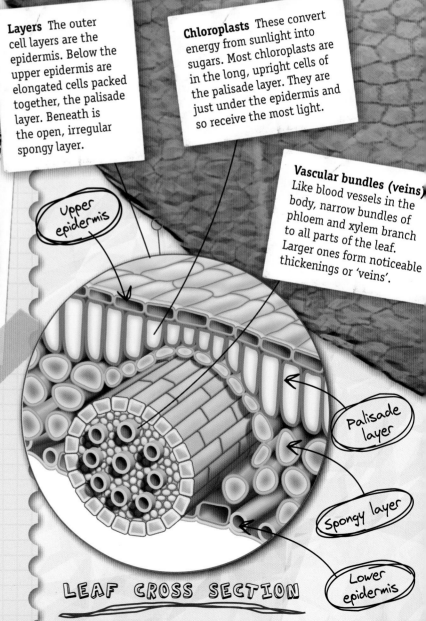

Upper epidermis

Palisade layer

Spongy layer

Lower epidermis

LEAF CROSS SECTION

To discover more about leaf anatomy and find fun activities to do visit www.factsforprojects.com and click on the web link.

✳ How does PHOTOSYNTHESIS work?

Photosynthesis means 'combining with light'. High-energy substances, especially sugars, are made from low-energy ingredients – water from the soil via the roots, and carbon dioxide from air. The resulting sugars are spread around the plant as sap, to be used for its daily life processes. Sugars are especially concentrated into the fruits of some plants to attract animals, so that seeds inside the fruits are spread. Oxygen is a byproduct.

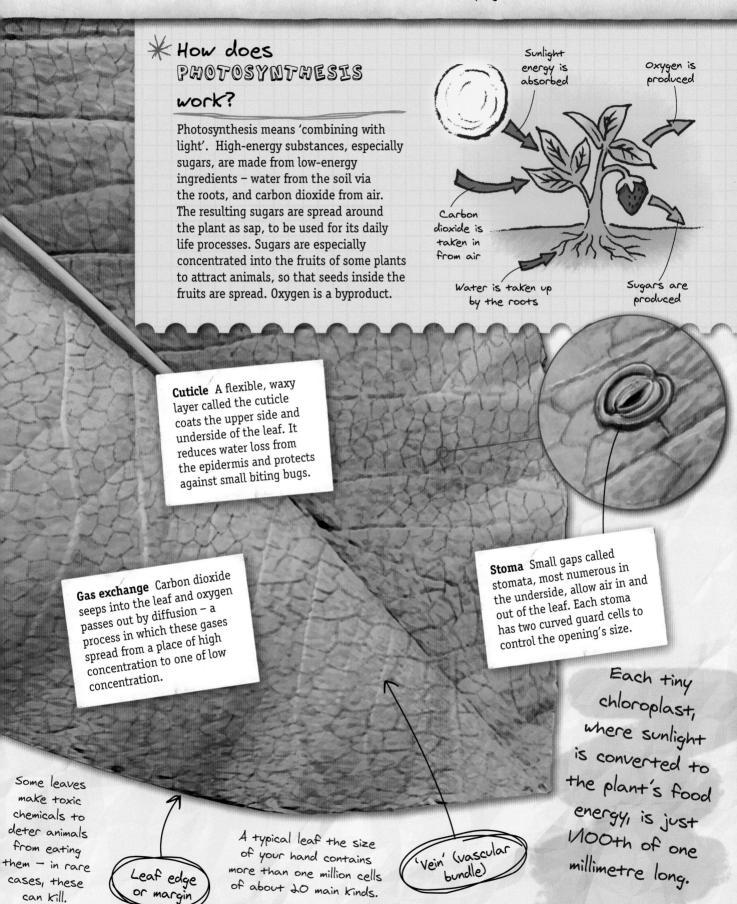

Sunlight energy is absorbed

Oxygen is produced

Carbon dioxide is taken in from air

Water is taken up by the roots

Sugars are produced

Cuticle A flexible, waxy layer called the cuticle coats the upper side and underside of the leaf. It reduces water loss from the epidermis and protects against small biting bugs.

Gas exchange Carbon dioxide seeps into the leaf and oxygen passes out by diffusion – a process in which these gases spread from a place of high concentration to one of low concentration.

Stoma Small gaps called stomata, most numerous in the underside, allow air in and out of the leaf. Each stoma has two curved guard cells to control the opening's size.

Each tiny chloroplast, where sunlight is converted to the plant's food energy, is just 1/100th of one millimetre long.

Some leaves make toxic chemicals to deter animals from eating them – in rare cases, these can kill.

Leaf edge or margin

A typical leaf the size of your hand contains more than one million cells of about 20 main kinds.

'Vein' (vascular bundle)

FLOWERS

Flowers only occur in certain plants – known as flowering plants or angiosperms. Such a plant could grow, live and survive without its flowers; some kinds can even reproduce without them. Most flowers are bisexual or 'perfect', containing both male and female parts. But these usually develop and ripen at different times, so a single flower is unlikely to breed with itself. Flowers with only female or only male parts are described as unisexual or 'imperfect'.

Did you know?

The first flowers probably appeared more than 130 million years ago, when dinosaurs were thriving. Their structure meant they were too soft to form fossils. However there are many excellent fossils of tiny, tough pollen grains that show flowers were around then.

If a plant is described as 'monoecious' it means there are separate female and male flowers on the same plant.

Colours The most brightly coloured petals belong to plants that attract insects for pollination. However many varieties are now bred artificially for bright colours.

✳ How are FLOWER PARTS arranged?

Plant experts study the detailed patterns and arrangements of flowers. Some flowers, such as lilies and grasses, have their parts arranged in multiples of three – sixes, nines and so on. Others are in multiples of four or five. This diagram shows an overhead view of one flower with the parts drawn in a simplified way in their positions. Studying flowers in this way helps scientists find out how flowers have evolved and developed, how we can help them to pollinate and breed new varieties, and even how certain fertilizers and pesticides will affect them.

Petals The petals are the second outermost parts, the outermost ones being the sepals. Petals may be entirely separate from each other. Or they may be joined at their bases to form a partial whorl, or joined all the way up their sides to give a deep trumpet shape.

ovule

Sepals (bud scales)

Carpel The egg cells are usually deep in the centre, in ovules inside the ovary. The female reproductive unit of stigma, style, ovary and ovules (sex cells) is the carpel.

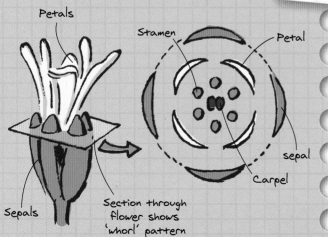

Petals

Stamen

Petal

sepal

Carpel

Sepals

Section through flower shows 'whorl' pattern

See amazing time-lapse footage of hawthorn blossom opening by visiting www.factsforprojects.com and clicking on the web link.

Style Extending from the ovary is a long style, which holds up a pad-like stigma to receive pollen grains. In the hibiscus flower shown here, the style (green) is inside the staminal column (red) bearing the stamens.

Filament holds up anther

Stigma

Anthers Each anther contains many thousands of pollen grains. Anthers only split or burst open when conditions are best for pollination.

If a plant is described as 'dioecious' it means that it is either female (with all female flowers) or male (bearing all male ones).

Among the most complicated flowers are orchids. Their three sepals and three petals have special colours and complex shapes, often to attract insects for better pollination.

Anther ready to release pollen

Stamen The male sex cells are inside tiny pollen grains. These are in bag-like anthers that grow on long stalks, the filaments. All these male parts are together known as stamens.

ovary

✳ RARE flowers

Most plants produce flowers once each year (annually), or perhaps every other year (biannually). But some have far longer flowering cycles. Certain cacti flower only after rain, which could be every 10–20 years. Various types of bamboo flower only every 50 or 100 years. Flowers also last varying amounts of time. The titan arum's huge bloom (below), which can reach 3 metres in height, grows after a gap of several years, yet shrivels and dies in just a few days.

Some plants have male, female and bisexual flowers all at the same time.

The foul-smelling 'corpse flower' may last only two days

POLLINATION

In spring and summer, millions of pollen grains float in the air – but most are far too small to see. These are windblown microscopic capsules containing male plant cells. There are so many capsules that some will land on the female part of a flower (or cone in conifers) of the same kind, so that the male cell can join with a female cell. This joining, called fertilization, will start the growth of a new seed.

Did you know?

Pollen grains are some of the toughest living structures. They can survive for thousands, even millions, of years. Pollen grains provide information about plant evolution, which plants lived where and climates long ago.

Apart from wind and animals, some plants use water to carry their pollen, such as elodea and other waterweeds.

Bee searches for nectar

Carriers As animal pollinators crawl and probe around a flower, pollen grains rub onto them from the open anthers, which are usually sticking up and 'in the way' of visitors.

1. POLLINATION

Hairy body gathers pollen grains

Colourful petals

Projecting anthers

✳ Lure of NECTAR

Pollen can be carried by wind, by animals or by water. Some flowers make a sweet fluid called nectar to lure creatures to drink from them, and in the process transfer pollen grains. For example, certain kinds of moths that have a long mouthpart called a proboscis, can reach the nectar in deep, trumpet-shaped flowers. While sipping, often when hovering in mid air, the moth is in exactly the right position to collect or deliver pollen.

Butterflies draw up flower nectar with their tubular mouthparts

Windblown pollen grains have been recorded in Antarctica from plants that are growing at least 5000 km away.

Read more about important animal pollinators and the plants they visit by going to www.factsforprojects.com and clicking on the web link.

The squash plant makes huge pollen grains that are about 1/4 of one millimetre across, just visible to the unaided eye.

Pumpkin pollen is one of the largest, and just about visible to the naked eye at 0.15 mm

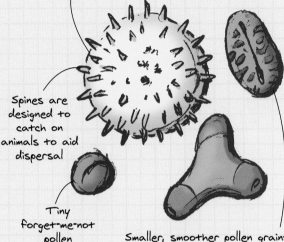

Spines are designed to catch on animals to aid dispersal

Tiny forget-me-not pollen

Smaller, smoother pollen grains are designed for wind dispersal

What does POLLEN look like?

At a quick glance, pollen grains look like fine pale or yellow dust – but only if there are thousands of them. Most individual grains are too small to see without a magnifier or microscope. Some have mini-spines or micro-hooks designed to catch onto the bodies of bees, beetles, birds, bats and similar creatures, which carry them to other flowers. Other grains have bubble-like parts, flaps or 'wings' to float well and blow in the breeze. Some pollen is so tiny and light that the slightest breath of wind carries it many kilometres.

Pollen grains on stigma

Style

Pollen tube When a pollen grain lands on the stigma, it grows a long, thin tube down the style. The male cell inside the grain travels down this to the female cell.

The biggest seeds are from the giant fan palm. Called coco-de-mer or double-coconuts, they weigh over 20 kg!

Fruits The fertilized cell grows into a tiny plant or embyro. Parts around it form its food storage and a seed case. In some plants there are also tasty, fleshy parts (see p19).

Seed in case

Ovary containing ovule

Male and female cells join

Tasty flesh for animals to eat

3. SEEDS AND FRUITS

2. FERTILIZATION

A single orchid bloom can release more than four million pollen grains.

GERMINATION

The genes inside a seed are programmed to begin germination only when the conditions are right. Then a plant will begin to grow. For many seeds this means warmth and moisture, which signal good growing conditions. Some need darkness too, showing they are in soil and have minerals and water. Others only germinate after a 'cold shock', which in nature is winter, and means that spring is on its way.

Did you know?

Seeds can stay viable – alive but dormant (inactive) and waiting to grow – for great spans of time. A date palm seed recovered from the ruins of an ancient palace, germinated and grew after a span of 2000 years.

Fleshy seed leaves called cotyledons contain food for growth

Seed coat or testa splits open

Radicle (first root)

The first shoot is called the plumule

A finch tucks into an autumn berry lunch

Runner bean seed
Inside is the embryo plant waiting to burst into life. Water soaks into the seed through the seed coat and also through a tiny hole, the micropyle, where the pollen tube entered.

✳ Berry BOUNTY

Plants do not make colourful, fleshy, tasty, snack-sized fruits and berries for fun. These structures attract animals that eat them. The animal gets a feast and also does the plant a favour. The seeds or pips inside the fruits have a tough casing that is not digested in the animal's gut. When the animal gets rid of the waste, the seeds drop into a new place far away from the parent plant, a process known as seed dispersal. The germinating seedlings do not compete with the parent for light, water and minerals, and they often they have excellent fertilizer in the form of the animal's droppings.

Radicle grows down

Stage 1 Even if the seed is upside down, the tiny new root, the radicle, is geotrophic – it reacts to the pull of gravity and grows straight downwards. The tiny shoot, or plumule, is phototrophic – it senses light and grows towards it.

Watch a time-lapse video clip of a bean germinating by visiting www.factsforprojects.com and clicking on the web link.

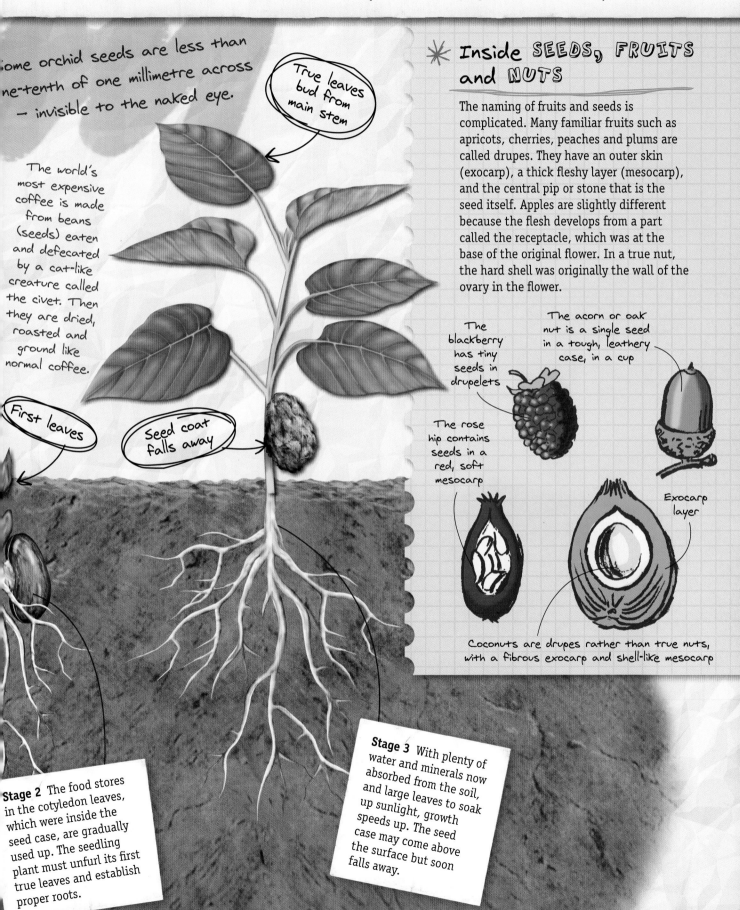

Some orchid seeds are less than one-tenth of one millimetre across — invisible to the naked eye.

True leaves bud from main stem

The world's most expensive coffee is made from beans (seeds) eaten and defecated by a cat-like creature called the civet. Then they are dried, roasted and ground like normal coffee.

First leaves

Seed coat falls away

✳ Inside SEEDS, FRUITS and NUTS

The naming of fruits and seeds is complicated. Many familiar fruits such as apricots, cherries, peaches and plums are called drupes. They have an outer skin (exocarp), a thick fleshy layer (mesocarp), and the central pip or stone that is the seed itself. Apples are slightly different because the flesh develops from a part called the receptacle, which was at the base of the original flower. In a true nut, the hard shell was originally the wall of the ovary in the flower.

The blackberry has tiny seeds in drupelets

The acorn or oak nut is a single seed in a tough, leathery case, in a cup

The rose hip contains seeds in a red, soft mesocarp

Exocarp layer

Coconuts are drupes rather than true nuts, with a fibrous exocarp and shell-like mesocarp

Stage 2 The food stores in the cotyledon leaves, which were inside the seed case, are gradually used up. The seedling plant must unfurl its first true leaves and establish proper roots.

Stage 3 With plenty of water and minerals now absorbed from the soil, and large leaves to soak up sunlight, growth speeds up. The seed case may come above the surface but soon falls away.

PLANT DEFENCES

Plants are sitting targets for all kinds of browsing, grazing and munching creatures, ranging from caterpillars to elephants. Some plants breed and grow well enough to remain common even when eaten in large numbers. Others defend themselves. They have spikes, prickles and thorns or may have foul-tasting or poisonous substances.

Did you know?

The creosote bush grows in the southwest deserts of North America. Its leaves make acrid-smelling poisonous chemicals that would kill most animals. Even so, a few bugs, caterpillars and grasshoppers have adapted to eating the leaves – and they smell of creosote too.

Flowers Cactus flowers may be on small accessory stems that branch from the main stem. In certain species they open for two hours, in others for weeks.

The tallest cacti are tree-like giant saguaros in southwest North America. Some are almost 20 m tall.

Flowers open after rain

✳ Danger, KEEP OFF!

It is a constant struggle for plants to develop adaptations that deter herbivorous animals, and for the herbivores to evolve means of getting past these defences. Acacia trees are dotted across the African plains, and their leaves are a tempting meal in this dry landscape. But the sharp, strong thorns repel most browsers. Ants make nests along the twigs too, and they attack any herbivores. Sometimes the giraffe, with its 50-centimetre-long tongue and thick-skinned lips, manages to grab a few mouthfuls.

Water storage In the prickly pear cactus, most of the water is in the swollen tissues around the stiffened central support.

Woody tissue Strong fibres form a central column to support the cactus and fix it to its extensive root system.

Giraffes carefully nibble leaves between the acacia tree's spines

To read more interesting facts about cacti and learn how to grow your own visit www.factsforprojects.com and click on the web link.

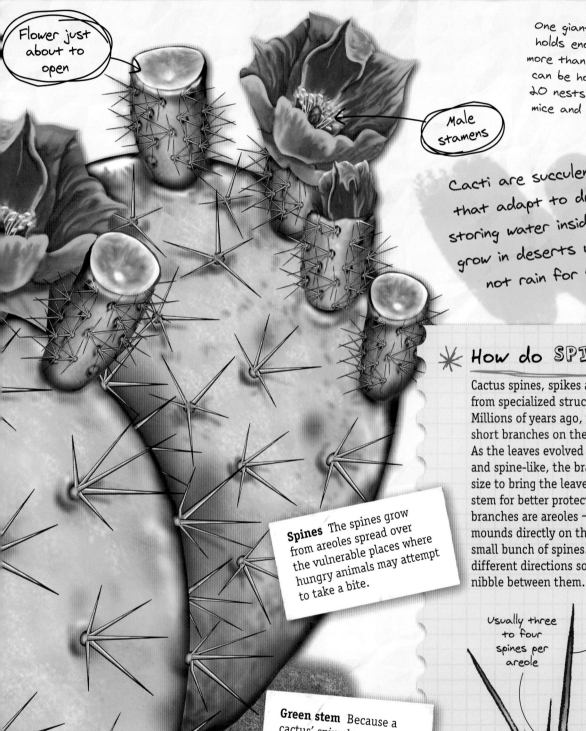

Flower just about to open

Male stamens

One giant saguaro cactus holds enough water to fill more than 20 bathtubs and can be home to more than 20 nests of birds, lizards, mice and other creatures.

Cacti are succulents — plants that adapt to dry regions by storing water inside. Some cacti grow in deserts where it does not rain for 50 years.

✳ How do SPINES work?

Cactus spines, spikes and thorns grow from specialized structures called areoles. Millions of years ago, these were probably short branches on the main cactus stem. As the leaves evolved to become thinner and spine-like, the branches shrank in size to bring the leaves closer to the juicy stem for better protection. Now these branches are areoles — small bumps or mounds directly on the stem, each with a small bunch of spines. These face out in different directions so an animal cannot nibble between them.

Spines The spines grow from areoles spread over the vulnerable places where hungry animals may attempt to take a bite.

Green stem Because a cactus' spiny leaves cannot carry out photosynthesis, the surface of the stem does so instead. The stem is a leaf-like green colour from its chlorophyll. Some types have ribs or flanges on the stem for extra surface area and strength.

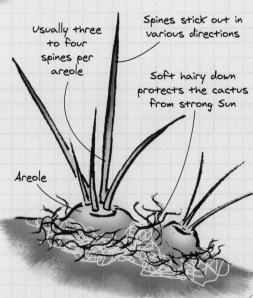

Usually three to four spines per areole

Spines stick out in various directions

Soft hairy down protects the cactus from strong Sun

Areole

CARNIVOROUS PLANTS

Carnivores eat meat – and some plants have taken to this way of life. They still need leaves to absorb sunlight for energy. However they live in very poor soil with few available nutrients for their roots to take in. So they get nourishment by catching, digesting and absorbing fluids and substances from small creatures, ranging from flies to frogs, lizards and mice.

Did you know?

One of the biggest carnivorous plants is the giant pitcher plant of Africa. Its jug-like vase grows to more than 40 centimetres in height and can hold more than 2 litres of digesting fluids. Despite this, some mosquitoes have adapted to using the pool to lay their eggs and breed.

Venus flytraps grow wild naturally in only a small area of southeastern USA.

✳ A sticky SOLUTION

There are several main kinds of carnivorous plant designs. The 'pitfall' type has a deep digesting container with slippery sides, as in the pitcher plant. The 'lobster-pot trap' is similar and has angled hairs pointing inwards to stop victims crawling out. The 'snap trap' uses fast leaf movements, as in the Venus flytrap. There is also the 'bladder' design that pops a balloon-like bladder that sucks in prey. The 'flypaper' version, like the sundew, has sticky flaps or blobs that adhere to victims.

Prey makes contact with trigger hairs

Trigger hairs The two leaf lobes only close if one hair is moved within 15–20 seconds of another, which helps to reduce 'false alarms'.

Leaf teeth Spiky teeth prevent big victims from struggling free, but also allow small ones, which are not worth digesting, to escape.

Central hinge joint or midrib

The sticky sundew plant claims another victim

Leaf stalk The Venus flytrap's killer leaves grow on strap-shaped leaf stalks, or petioles, which have enough surface area to carry out photosynthesis.

See a Venus flytrap in action by visiting
www.factsforprojects.com and clicking on the web link.

A healthy Venus flytrap can snap shut in half a second.

Trapped fly

Lobe teeth interlock

Closed trap Once two or more hairs are moved, the two leaf lobes snap shut in less than a second. The more the victim wriggles, the tighter the lobes press together. The leaf remains closed for about a week.

How do TRIGGER HAIRS work?

Scientists still do not know exactly how the flytrap works in terms of chemical changes within the leaf. However the key seems to be a 'flip' in the lobes, from their normal out-curved or concave shape on the outer surface, to an in-curved or convex shape after triggering. It seems that the fast intake of water by cells on the outer surface makes them expand to flick the shape of the lobe so it curves the opposite way

Trigger hairs

Fly victim

Out-curved outer surface

Rapid expansion of the outer layer causes the lobes to 'flip' and curve inwards

Digestion As the victim dies, tiny glands on the inner surfaces of the leaf lobes begin to ooze digestive juices. These seep into the prey and turn its soft flesh into a pulp of nutrients, which soak into the leaf.

Leaf stalk

Cutaway view

Bug is slowly dissolved over ten days

Digestive glands

PARASITIC PLANTS

A parasite is an organism that lives in or on another living thing – the host. By living off a host, a parasite can gain food and shelter, but usually at a cost to the host. Plants are no exception. They can parasitize other plants, moulds or fungi, and even animals. Often they do not kill the host. This ensures there will be more hosts to provide for the parasite's future generations.

Did you know?

The mysterious, ghostly-looking broomrape plant has long been linked to witchcraft. It has no leaves and its roots steal nourishment from host plants around. Only the pale stem shows above ground with its small flowers. Eating this plant was said to give special powers, such as being able to cast spells.

Mistletoe occasionally grows independently in very rich, well-watered soil.

Mistletoe is fine for birds to eat but poisonous to humans – no part of the plant should be eaten.

✳ How MISTLETOE grows

In autumn and winter, juicy mistletoe berries are magnets for wild animals, especially birds such as the mistle thrush. The birds swallow the berries and excrete the seeds in their droppings on branches, ready to germinate. Or they squeeze the sticky, juicy parts off the seed and swallow them, then wipe their beaks on a branch or twig and transfer the seed there. A very tacky substance called viscin in the remaining berry pulp dries and sets hard, keeping the seed attached long enough to germinate and develop its haustorium (see right).

Berries The young berries are green at first, then gradually turn yellow and finally ripen to pearly-white to attract hungry creatures. The speed of ripening depends mainly on exposure to sunshine.

More than 500 kinds of trees and bushes are known to be parasitized by about 80 different kinds of mistletoes found around the world.

Host Many kinds of trees are suitable hosts for mistletoe, including apple and related fruit trees, and also lime, poplar trees and hawthorns.

Host branch

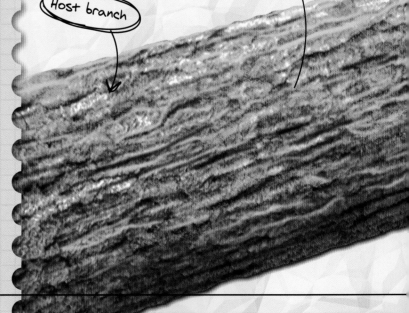

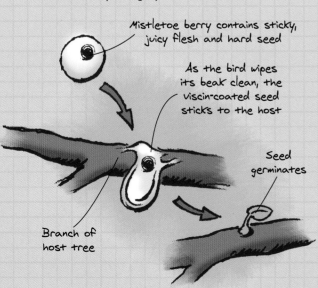

Mistletoe berry contains sticky, juicy flesh and hard seed

As the bird wipes its beak clean, the viscin-coated seed sticks to the host

Seed germinates

Branch of host tree

Discover more about parasitic plants around the world by visiting www.factsforprojects.com and clicking on the web link.

✳ Real big SUCKER

Parasitic plants can thrive in the gloom of dense rainforests because they do not need leaves to catch sunlight energy. Intead they parasitize the roots of trailing vines or trees. The biggest single flower in the world – the rafflesia is one example. This grows in the rainforests of Southeast Asia. It is little more than a root-like haustorium that occasionally develops one huge bloom that can be up to one metre across. The bloom gives off the scent of rotting meat to attract flesh flies and other insects that usually lay their eggs on rotting animal carcasses. These insects are the flower's pollinators.

Leaves Mistletoe is a hemi-parasite (partial parasite). It gains water and minerals from the host, but produces its own energy-rich foods by photosynthesis in its leaves.

Mistletoe is an evergreen. Its leaves often stand out in winter on broad-leaved deciduous trees that have lost their leaves in autumn.

Original seed position

Haustorium This root-like structure invades the host tree's branch, sending finger-like projections into its vessels to get water and minerals coming up from the roots. The host's leaves can photosynthesize as normal.

The huge rafflesia is a parasitic plant

Woody growth rings in host branch

Xylem The haustorium invade the host's xylem vessels and divert water and minerals into themselves. For a big host, this does little harm.

Path of mineral nutrients and water

For centuries, mistletoe has been regarded as a magical plant. It was often associated with love and fertility.

SEAWEEDS

Seaweeds are varied kinds of larger plants called algae that grow in the sea, rather than a single plant group. Most live along rocky shores where their tough, leathery parts cope with the tidal cycle, being submerged and then left in air, and also winds and waves. These plants have no flowers and no real leaves, stems or roots. The main body (thallus) soaks up minerals and carries out photosynthesis over most of its surface.

Did you know?

Giant kelp, a brown seaweed, is one of the biggest and fastest-growing seaweeds. In one year it can reach a length of 50 metres, supported by the water around it. In the best growing conditions it increases in length by half a metre per day. These kelp form waving underwater 'forests' that are home to huge numbers of animals.

On very exposed shores, bladderwrack has no bladders.

✳ Undersea RETREAT

Green seaweeds include sea lettuce and gut weed. Kelps, wracks and thongweed are known as brown seaweeds, while laver, dulse and carragheen are red seaweeds. These plants provide food for many creatures, from tiny sea snails to large fish. They are also a great place to shelter from the waves, wind and sun, and to hide from predators. Sea otters float in kelp beds and wrap themselves in the fronds as they rest and sleep.

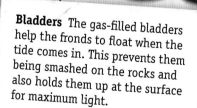

Bladders The gas-filled bladders help the fronds to float when the tide comes in. This prevents them being smashed on the rocks and also holds them up at the surface for maximum light.

The sea otter hunts for shellfish in a kelp bed

An extract of seaweed called agar is used in cooking to thicken all kinds of foods, from soups to jellies and ice cream.

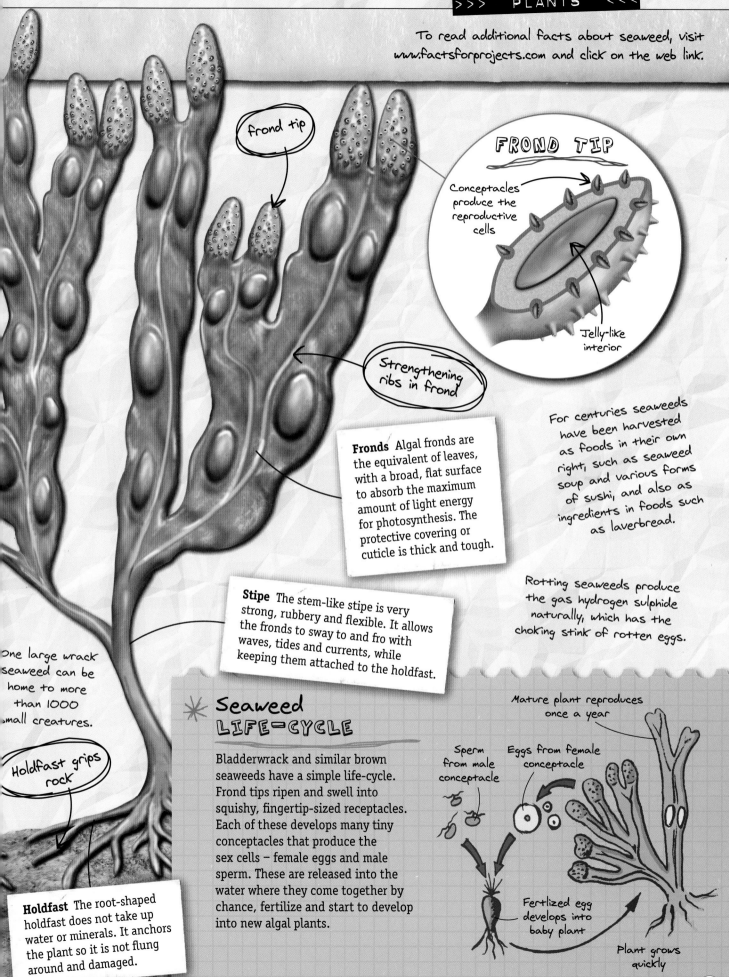

To read additional facts about seaweed, visit www.factsforprojects.com and click on the web link.

frond tip

FROND TIP

Conceptacles produce the reproductive cells

Jelly-like interior

Strengthening ribs in frond

For centuries seaweeds have been harvested as foods in their own right, such as seaweed soup and various forms of sushi, and also as ingredients in foods such as laverbread.

Fronds Algal fronds are the equivalent of leaves, with a broad, flat surface to absorb the maximum amount of light energy for photosynthesis. The protective covering or cuticle is thick and tough.

Rotting seaweeds produce the gas hydrogen sulphide naturally, which has the choking stink of rotten eggs.

Stipe The stem-like stipe is very strong, rubbery and flexible. It allows the fronds to sway to and fro with waves, tides and currents, while keeping them attached to the holdfast.

One large wrack seaweed can be home to more than 1000 small creatures.

Holdfast grips rock

Seaweed LIFE-CYCLE

Bladderwrack and similar brown seaweeds have a simple life-cycle. Frond tips ripen and swell into squishy, fingertip-sized receptacles. Each of these develops many tiny conceptacles that produce the sex cells – female eggs and male sperm. These are released into the water where they come together by chance, fertilize and start to develop into new algal plants.

Mature plant reproduces once a year

Sperm from male conceptacle

Eggs from female conceptacle

Fertlized egg develops into baby plant

Plant grows quickly

Holdfast The root-shaped holdfast does not take up water or minerals. It anchors the plant so it is not flung around and damaged.

27

MOSS

Mosses are just about the simplest plants on land. They have no flowers, no true roots or complex leaves, and no tiny vessels inside to form stiff stems to carry around water and sap. Mosses are soft and must live in damp places, usually near the ground, in the shade where it stays relatively cool. They have to soak up water all over, which puts a limit on their size.

Did you know?

Peat-bog or sphagnum moss is very springy and spongy, even after being dried. For centuries people used it as a sponge for washing. Dry sphagnum was also useful as a dressing for wounds, since it soaks up blood and fluids well, and also contains substances that kill germs.

Spore cap Known as the operculum, the cap of the capsule detaches in fine weather when spores are most likely to carry on the breeze.

Clubmosses look like large mosses but they are more closely related to ferns.

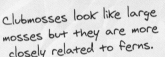

Ripening capsule

Mosses are scientifically known as bryophytes. They rarely grow more than about 10 cm tall, yet there are more than 12,000 species.

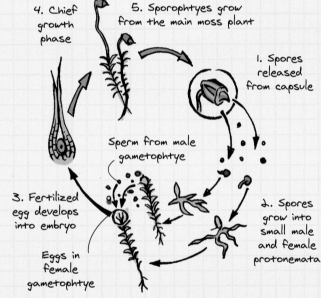

4. Chief growth phase

5. Sporophtyes grow from the main moss plant

1. Spores released from capsule

Sperm from male gametophtye

3. Fertilized egg develops into embryo

Eggs in female gametophtye

2. Spores grow into small male and female protonemata

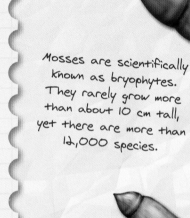

Young capsule

✳ Shedding SPORES

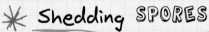

A moss plant has a complex life-cycle with two main stages: gametophyte and sporophyte. The sporophyte stage grows from the gametophyte, which is the main leafy plant. Its spore capsules release spores, which are like seeds but lack food reserves. If the spores germinate they develop into tiny thread-like plants called protonemata. These lead to the gametophyte stage. Gametophytes produce tiny stalks that make gametes (male sperm and female eggs) at their tips. The sperm swim to the eggs in water (which is why mosses live in damp places), and fertilize them. The fertilized eggs develop into sporophytes, and the cycle continues.

Leaflets The small leaflets may be slightly lobed or serrated. They carry out photosynthesis, but the energy-containing foods they produce pass around the plant by seepage or diffusion, rather than along phloem vessels (tubes). This is the gametophyte stage of the life-cycle.

Read interesting facts about mosses by visiting www.factsforprojects.com and clicking on the web link.

Mosses are regarded as weeds in many lawns, but are highly valued in Japanese gardens.

Spores shaken out

Liverworts reproduce in the same way as mosses

* Weird BREEDERS

Liverworts are close relatives of mosses. They have a broad, flat main body called a thallus that resembles the human liver, hence the name. Liverworts breed in the same way as mosses, by spores. But their life-cycles are opposite to other plants and to animals. In a typical plant or animal, the female egg cell and male sperm cell each have one set of genes. They join to make a fertilized egg, which has a double set of genes and grows into the adult. In mosses and liverworts, the adult, the actual plant, has only one set of genes. The phase of the life-cycle with two sets of genes is much smaller and rarely noticed.

Spore capsule Each capsule is a container for hundreds or thousands of microscopic spores, which will grow into the other stage of the life-cycle, gametophyte.

Receptacle

In northern regions, the north-facing sides of trees and rocks are usually most shady and damp, so have most moss growth. It's the reverse in the Southern Hemisphere.

Leaflets grow in whorls

Spore stalk The stalk lengthens as the spore capsule ripens, to 1–3 centimetres long. This raises the capsule above the leaflet mass and into the wind, for better spore distribution. This is the sporophyte stage of the life-cycle.

Rhizoids These look like roots, but have little internal structure. They serve mainly to fix the moss to rock or bark. The rhizoids also grow and spread to extend the moss. They soak up water too, as do the leaflets and the rest of the plant.

FERNS

Ferns lack flowers, but they have most other parts of a complex plant, such as leaves, stems and roots. In particular they contain tiny tube-like vessels to carry water and other substances around the whole plant, so they are known as vascular plants. Lacking flowers, they have no seeds and reproduce by means of spores.

Did you know?

About 300 million years ago the hot, steamy Carboniferous forests were thick with ancient relatives of mosses and ferns. They included scale trees, club mosses, giant ferns, seed ferns and tree ferns. Some were over 50 metres tall. Nearly all kinds became extinct as conifer trees and then blossom trees took over the land.

Fossils of chewed-up ferns have been found with the remains of dinosaurs from over 200 million years ago.

Stipelet (secondary stem)

Fronds Fern leaves or fronds are among the most complicated in the plant world. The main stem branches into secondary stems, which bear leaf parts called pinnae, which are subdivided into pinnules.

The silver fern of New Zealand appears on the nation's coat of arms and the badge of their All Blacks rugby team.

Early frond

Water ferns can choke canals, lakes and rivers

✳ Fern INVADERS!

Some ferns are a real menace. The floating mosquito fern, or azolla, is hardly the size of a fingernail. But it multiplies so fast, simply by splitting in two, that within weeks it can cover a huge area of water. It stops light getting to other plants and chokes fish and other animals. Bracken is a tall, tough fern that spreads rapidly by its rhizomes. Introduced into new regions, it soon invades natural habitats such as wood edges, meadows and shrubland.

FROND UNDERSIDE

Sorus (cluster of sporangia)

Find out more about where ferns grow, how they develop and the threats they face by visiting www.factsforprojects.com and clicking on the web link.

Pinnules (small leaf divisions)

✳ Making more FERNS

The fern's life-cycle is similar in some ways to the moss life-cycle. It has a large plant stage, the familiar fern, which is the sporophyte or spore-making stage. This alternates with a very small plant stage, the prothallus, which is the gametophyte stage and makes the eggs and sperm (sex cells). But the genetics of the fern are more similar to other plants, and the other way around from the moss. The stage of the life-cycle with one set of genes (haploid) is the small and rarely noticed prothallus (gametophyte), while the stage with two sets of genes (diploid) is the main fern plant.

Sporangia All fronds carry out photosynthesis in the usual way. However only certain fronds, called sporophylls, develop the spore-producing sporangia.

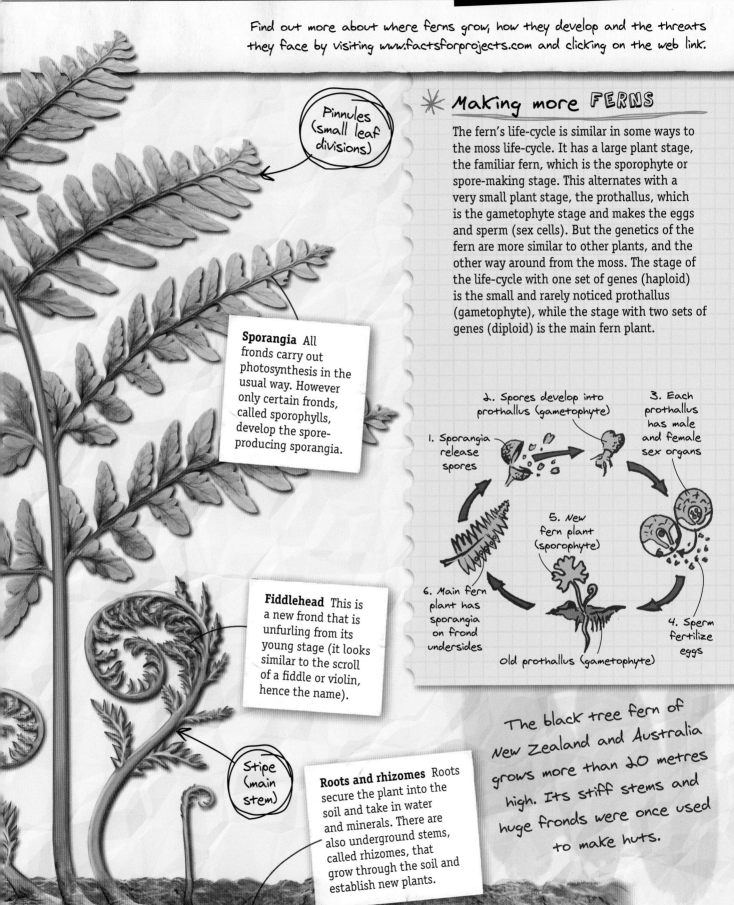

1. Sporangia release spores

2. Spores develop into prothallus (gametophyte)

3. Each prothallus has male and female sex organs

5. New fern plant (sporophyte)

6. Main fern plant has sporangia on frond undersides

4. Sperm fertilize eggs

Old prothallus (gametophyte)

Fiddlehead This is a new frond that is unfurling from its young stage (it looks similar to the scroll of a fiddle or violin, hence the name).

Stipe (main stem)

Roots and rhizomes Roots secure the plant into the soil and take in water and minerals. There are also underground stems, called rhizomes, that grow through the soil and establish new plants.

The black tree fern of New Zealand and Australia grows more than 20 metres high. Its stiff stems and huge fronds were once used to make huts.

CONIFERS

Conifers are gymnosperms – plants with seeds that grow in woody cones rather than in flowers. Most coniferous trees have needle- or scale-like leaves that stay on the tree all year, so we call them evergreens. The conifer group includes pines, firs, spruces, redwoods, cypresses, hemlocks, larches (which are not evergreen) and yews (which have berry-like cones). The tallest, heaviest and oldest living thing on Earth is a conifer.

Did you know?

The biggest living things in the world are giant redwood trees growing along the west coasts of North America. A redwood called General Sherman is 84 metres tall and probably weighs more than 2000 tonnes, which is 20 times heavier than the biggest blue whale.

The world's tallest tree is a conifer – a 115-m-tall coast redwood in California, USA.

Branches and twigs In most conifers the branches emerge from one central trunk – they do not have branching crowns like broadleaved trees.

Conifer needles are so tough that in cold regions they can take more than 100 years to rot away (broad leaves take a few months).

ANTI-FREEZE

Most conifer trees grow in cool and cold places, especially around the north of North America, northern Europe and northern Asia. Here they form boreal forests covering vast areas. Their narrow, strong leaves have thick coatings and can withstand being deep-frozen for months during the long winter. Also, the tree branches tend to slope down so that snow slides off them easily, and the bark is thick and stringy to resist frost. Boreal forests are among the biggest unexplored places left on Earth.

Needles Each needle has tiny versions of the sap (phloem) and water (xylem) vessels found in broad leaves. There are also tubes for sticky scented resins, which the tree makes to help repel animals and seal damage caused by teeth or claws.

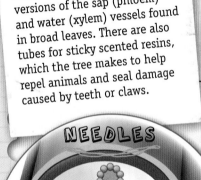

NEEDLES

Water and sap vessels

Resin vessels

Stoma (air gap)

Most conifers keep their leaves all year round

Some cones only release seeds when scorched by a forest fire. This may be years after seed production.

Read facts and view pictures and videos of conifers by visiting www.factsforprojects.com and clicking on the web link.

The sugar pine tree of western North America produces female cones that can be more than 65 cm long. The wings of their seeds measure 3 cm across.

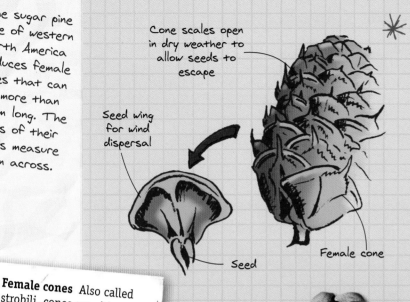

Cone scales open in dry weather to allow seeds to escape

Seed wing for wind dispersal

Seed

Female cone

How do CONES work?

Cones are the woody equivalent of flowers in blossom trees – they produce seeds. Most conifers are monoecious, with one tree having both female and male cones. The male cones usually take between one and two years to mature, then open to release their windblown pollen grains containing the male sex cells. Likewise female cones take up to three years to mature, then receive pollen grains. The male cells fertilize the female egg cells, which develop into embryo plants inside seeds. Many conifer seeds have wings to blow away and disperse on the wind. Conifers such as junipers and yews have juicy berries that encourage animals to spread their seeds.

Female cones Also called strobili, cones are either male or female. Female cones are larger and more woody. They are usually higher up the tree, to avoid being pollinated by their tree's pollen from below.

Released pollen

Male cones The male cones are smaller and softer than the female ones, and tend to rot or disintegrate faster. Their segments are known as scales and pollen is released from between them.

Main twig

BROADLEAVED PLANTS

Most broadleaved plants have broad leaves – but not all. The term 'broadleaved' is used to describe flowering plants that have seeds that are made in flowers, to distinguish them from needle-leaved conifers whose seeds are made in cones. Broadleaved plants are the most successful and numerous plants in the world. There are over 250,000 different kinds. As grasses, herbs, flowers, shrubs, bushes and trees, they dominate almost all habitats except for the coldest places.

Did you know?

Grasses do not look like broad-leaved flowering plants, but they are. Their seeds, in the form of grains, are the main source of basic food for the vast majority of people in the world – rice, wheat, rye, oats, maize (sweetcorn), barley, sugarcane and sorghum are some examples.

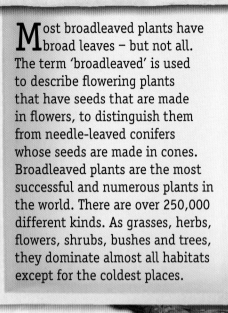

Heartwood At the centre of the trunk is the oldest, dead xylem from the tree's early years, strengthened with woody fibres of lignin.

Main bough

The English (or pedunculate) oak grows across Europe and also in parts of North America. It can grow to 50 m tall, reach 1500 years of age and produce more than 100,000 acorns (nuts) each year.

Bark The tree's 'skin' helps protect against small bugs, bigger browsing animals and extreme temperatures.

Phloem vessels These sap-conducting tubes are just under the bark, in a soft, pale layer.

Xylem vessels More water-carrying tubes are added beneath the bark each year, leaving annual growth rings.

Roots The roots lengthen downwards and sideways every year. In a healthy tree they may occupy a volume equal to the size of the crown.

Primary root

Download a leaf identification sheet and tick off the broadleaved plants you spot by visiting www.factsforprojects.com and clicking on the web link.

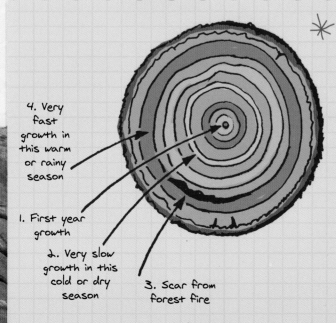

Leaves Oaks are deciduous, so the leaves will shrivel, die and fall in autumn. The tree withdraws nourishment from them as they die, to store in the woody parts and new buds.

Branches The branches and twigs form the part known as the crown. The oak usually has a spreading, irregular, lumpy-looking crown.

Lobed leaf shape

Tree rings show that the oldest broadleaved trees include several types of figs. One carefully tended sacred fig is calculated to be over 2200 years of age.

A single English oak may be home to more than 500 kinds of animals, from wood-boring grubs to tawny owls.

Upside-down trees?

Broadleaved trees have a huge range of shapes and sizes to adapt to their particular habitats. In the far north, tiny Arctic dwarf willow trees grow small and low, to stay below the worst of the freezing winds. In dry areas, baobab trees and others have wide trunks that store thousands of litres of water taken up by their deep, spreading root systems. They also have just a small crown of branches and leaves on top, to prevent losing water through the leaves.

These huge baobab trees are growing on the African plains

4. Very fast growth in this warm or rainy season

1. First year growth

2. Very slow growth in this cold or dry season

3. Scar from forest fire

How do TREE RINGS form?

Trees grow in two ways. Primary growth is length – roots, branches and twigs lengthen at their tips. Secondary growth is width as the trunk, branches and twigs thicken. This happens under the bark. A very thin layer called the cambium produces new phloem on its outside, just beneath the bark, and new xylem inside. As layers of woody xylem build up each year, they expand the whole diameter, with cambium and phloem still on the outside. Fast growth in spring-summer or the rainy season forms the wider part of one ring, and slow growth at other times the narrow part. Good years have wider rings.

RAINFORESTS

Nowhere on Earth are plants so numerous and varied as in tropical rainforests. Year-round warmth, moisture and strong sunlight between the clouds are ideal conditions for a riot of growth and colour. Plants here also have amazingly intricate relationships with each other, such as parasites and hosts, and a myriad of animals spread their pollen and seeds far and wide.

Did you know?

Tropical rainforests are home to almost half the world's plant and animal species. They are by far the most biodiverse of all habitats. A rainforest may have 100 times more plant species, and 1000 times more animal species, than a forest in a dry, cool temperate region.

Rainforests have more orchid species than all other habitats combined.

Spider monkey Animals such as monkeys, sloths and snakes may spend their entire lives in the canopy and hardly ever touch the ground.

Dangling liana

Creeper on trunk

Clouds form in the humid air above a rainforest

Over half of the world's tropical forests have been cut down in the past 100 years. The rest may disappear in another 50 years.

Some rainforest vines have trailing stems 200 m long.

Buttress roots

✳ MOTHER of forests

Tropical rainforest trees are far more than homes for animals. Their tree roots take up the huge amounts of water that fall as rain, and gradually release it as vapour through the leaves. This creates clouds and affects the climate hundreds of kilometres away. The leaves also produce huge amounts of oxygen by photosynthesis, which keeps our air fresh. The roots hold the soil in place so it is not washed away by rainstorms to choke rivers.

To discover more amazing information about the layers of the rainforest visit www.factsforprojects.com and click on the web link.

Emergents Huge trees called emergents rise above the canopy and form the overstorey. They can be 80 metres tall and 30 metres wide – ideal lookouts for eagles, owls and monkeys.

Flowers that grow on other plants for support are called epiphytes.

Main canopy The dense tangle of twigs, buds, leaves, flowers and fruits is home to up to nine-tenths of rainforest life. It is generally 5–10 metres deep and on average about 20–40 metres above the ground.

Main trunk

Buttress flange

Buttress root

Shallow soil layer

Alexandra's birdwing butterfly

How do BUTTRESS ROOTS work?

Surprisingly, the soil of tropical forests is thin and not especially nourishing. Fallen wood, leaves and fruits rot quickly in the damp warmth and are recycled rapidly into new tree growth, so deep, rich soil cannot build up. To keep upright in these conditions, some rainforest trees have buttress roots. They are flanges that extend sideways from the trunk to make the base of the tree wider. They give better stability and also help to take up more minerals in the competitive struggle against neighbouring trees.

Understorey Bushes, shrubs and small trees below the canopy compete for light and space. They may get a chance to grow taller when a great tree dies.

Strangler figs grow stems around a host tree, then envelop and kill it.

Forest floor It is gloomy and quiet at ground level. Only specialized herbs, creepers, mosses and ferns grow here.

Tree frog

37

GLOSSARY

Angiosperm
A group of flowering plants that reproduce using male and female parts (stamens and carpels) that form seeds.

Carpel
The female reproductive unit of a seed-making plant, including the stigma, style and ovary organs.

Chlorophyll
The light-catching, green pigment found in most plants, especially in the leaves.

Chloroplasts
Parts of plant cells that contain chlorophyll to turn sunlight energy into energy-rich sugars and similar products, by the process of photosynthesis. They may be shaped like discs, eggs or sausages.

Cuticle
A flexible, waxy layer covering various parts of a plant, especially the leaves and buds. It usually protects and keeps in moisture while keeping out extremes of temperature.

Deciduous
Plants that lose their leaves, usually at a certain time each year, such as at the start of the cold or dry season. The leaves are regrown when conditions improve.

Dormant
Seeds that are still alive, but inactive or 'sleeping'. They are waiting for suitable conditions in which to grow, such as warmth and moisture.

Whorl pattern

Drupe
A fruit with an outer skin or exocarp, a thick fleshy layer or mesocarp, and a central pip or stone that is the seed itself, such as a cherry or peach.

Embryo plant
A tiny, early version of a plant, usually inside a seed or spore.

Epidermis
The covering layer of cells on a living thing or its parts, for example, on a leaf.

Flower
The parts of a flowering plant that are specialized for reproduction by producing seeds, bearing the female sex parts (carpels), the male sex parts (stamens), or both.

Fruits
Parts of a plant that contain its seeds, which were formed from the ovaries. Nuts and berries are fruits.

Gametophyte
The stage in the life cycle of certain plants that produces the sex cells or gametes (male sperm and female eggs).

Geotrophic
Reacting to the pull of gravity and growing towards (or away from) it.

Germinate
When a plant starts to grow from its seed, usually sending out roots and a shoot to form a young plant called a seedling.

Heartwood
The oldest, dead, lignin-strengthened xylem from a tree's early years, found at the centre of its trunk and large branches.

Hermaphrodite
A plant that has flowers with both female and male parts in each flower, also called bisexual or 'perfect'.

Lignin
The main substance that forms tough, strong, stiff fibres in the woody parts of plants, especially the trunks and branches of bushes and trees.

Monoecious
Having separate female and male flowers on the same plant.

Nut
A seed with a hard shell formed from what was originally the wall of the ovary in the flower.

Ovary
Part of a plant that contains the female reproductive sex cells, or egg cells, plus their associated cells – sometimes called ovules.

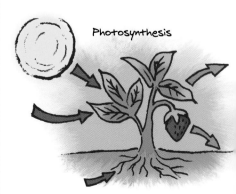

Photosynthesis

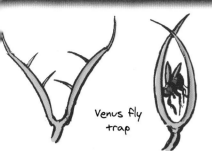

Venus fly trap

Palisade layer

The main photosynthetic layer of cells in a leaf, usually formed from lots of upright, elongated cells packed closely together.

Parasite

A living thing that gains something from another living thing, called the host, such as food or shelter, while harming the host in the process.

Petals

The second outermost parts in a typical flower. They may be small and inconspicuous or, more usually, large and brightly coloured.

Petiole

The stalk of a leaf, which can be either very long or very short.

Phloem

Tube-like vessels that carry liquids rich in glucose (sugars) and other nutrients made by photosynthesis, usually from the leaves to other parts of a vascular plant.

Photosynthesis

Using the energy in sunlight and converting it into chemical substances, chiefly high-energy sugars such as glucose, to power life processes. It is the major feature of plants and makes them primary producers.

Pollination

The transfer of pollen grains containing sex cells from the male parts of a flower to the female parts of a flower of the same kind. Pollen is usually transferred by wind or animals, depending on the type of plant.

Primary producer

A living thing that obtains energy from a source that is not another living thing. Plants are the main group, trapping energy from sunlight.

Rhizoids

Root-like parts that help to secure a plant in position, and perhaps soak up water and minerals, but without the organized inner structure and vessels of true roots.

Roots

The part of a plant with an organized internal structure and vessels that take in water and usually minerals. Often underground, roots also help keep the plant in position.

Seed

An embryo or tiny early version of a plant, along with food stores, in a protective casing.

Sepals

The outermost parts in a typical flower, often forming green protective 'covers' around the rest of the flower when it is still a bud.

Spore

An embryo of a plant (or a fungus, germ or similar living thing) in a protective casing but without any food stores.

Sporophyte

The stage in the life cycle of certain plants that makes the spores, from which the next stage (gametophyte) will grow.

Stamen

The male reproductive unit of a seed-making plant, including pollen grains containing sex cells, in the anther on its stalk-like filament.

Stomata

Small gaps in the surface of some plants, especially on the undersides of leaves, that allow air in and out of the leaf, so that carbon dioxide can be obtained for photosynthesis.

Succulents

Plants that adapt to dry regions by storing water in their leaves, stems, roots or other parts.

Vascular plant

A plant with well-formed tubes or vessels, such as phloem and xylem, for transporting liquids around the plant.

Xylem

Usually stiff, pipe-like vessels that carry water with dissolved minerals from the soil to most parts of a vascular plant.

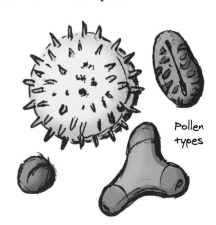

Pollen types

INDEX

acacias 20
acorns 19, 34
Africa 9, 20, 22, 35
agar 26
air 8, 13, 16, 22, 26, 36
algae 26–27
angiosperms 14, 34
animals 8, 10, 13, 14, 15, 16, 17, 18, 20, 21, 22, 23, 24, 25, 26, 29, 30, 32, 33, 34, 35, 36, 37
anthers 15, 16
apples 19, 24
Arctic dwarf willow tree 35
areoles 21
Asia 32
aspen tree 10
Australia 31
autumn 24, 25, 35

bamboo 15
baobab trees 35
bark 32, 34, 35
bees 16, 17
berries 18, 24, 33
birds 17, 18, 21, 24
black tree fern 31
blackberries 19
bladderwrack 26, 27
blossom 15, 30, 33, 34
boreal forests 32
boughs 34
bracken 30
branches 21, 24, 25, 32, 35
breeding 14, 20, 22, 29
broad-leaved plants 25, 32, **34–35**
broomrape plant 24
bryophytes 28
buds 8, 9, 14, 19, 35, 37
bugs 12, 20, 23, 34
bushes 8, 24, 34, 37
butterflies 16, 37
buttress roots 36, 37

cacti 15, 20, 21
cambium 35
canopy 36, 37
carbon dioxide 12, 13
Carboniferous forests 30
carnivorous plants **22–23**
carpels 14
caterpillars 20
cells 8, 9, 10, 11, 12, 13, 14, 17, 23, 28
chemical energy 12
chlorophyll 12, 21
chloroplasts 9, 12, 13
climate 16, 36
clouds 36
coconuts 19
coffee 19
colours 14, 15, 36
conceptacles 27
cones 32, 33, 34
conifer trees 30, **32–33**, 34
cortex 10
cotyledons 18, 19

creepers 36, 37
creosote bush 20
crown 34, 35
cuticles 10, 12, 27
cytoplasm 9

dangling liana 36
date palm 18
deciduous trees 25, 35
defences **20–21**
deserts 9, 20, 21
diffusion 13, 28
digestion 22, 23
dioecious plants 15
diploid stage 29, 31
drupes 19

eggs 14, 15, 22, 25, 27, 28, 29, 30, 31, 33
embryos 17, 18, 33
emergents 37
endoplasmic reticulum 9
energy 8, 9, 12, 13, 22, 25, 28
epidermis 10, 11, 12
epiphytes 37
Europe 32, 34
evergreens 25, 32
evolution 14, 16, 20
exocarps 19

female cells 17, 28, 29
female cones 33
female parts 14, 16
ferns 29, **30–31**, 37
fertilization 16, 17, 27, 28, 31, 33
fertilizers 14, 18
fibres 8, 9, 10, 20, 34
fiddleheads 31
figs 35
filaments 15
flies 22, 23, 25
floating mosquito ferns 30
flowers 8, 9, **14–15**, 16, 17, 19, 20, 21, 24, 25, 34, 37
food 13, 17, 18, 19, 24, 25, 26, 28, 34
fossils 14, 30
frogs 22, 37
fronds 26, 27, 30, 31
fruits 13, 17, 18, 19, 24, 37
fungi 24

gamete-producing stage 28
gametophyte stage 28, 31
gas exchange 13
gases 8, 26
General Sherman (tree) 32
genes 18, 29, 31
germination **18–19**, 24, 28
giant fan palm 17
giant kelp 26
giant pitcher plant 22
giant redwoods 32

giant saguaros 20, 21
giant waterlily 12
giraffes 20
golgi bodies 9
grasses 8, 14, 34
grazing 20

haploid stage 29, 31
haustorium 24, 25
heartwood 34
herbivorous animals 8, 10, 20
herbs 8, 34, 37
hermaphrodite plants 14
hibiscus 15
holdfasts 27
hosts 24, 25, 36, 37
hydrogen sulphide 27

insects 14, 15, 25

leaflets 28, 29
leaves 8, 9, 11, **12–13**, 18, 19, 20, 21, 22, 23, 25, 30, 32, 33, 35, 36, 37
life-cycles 27, 29, 31
light 8, 10, 12, 13, 18, 26, 27, 30
lignin 10, 34
lilies 14
liverworts 29
lizards 21, 22

main stems 9, 10, 19, 30, 31
male cones 33
male parts 14, 15, 21
male cells 16, 17
mesocarps 19
mice 21, 22
microbes 10
micropyles 18
minerals 8, 9, 10, 11, 18, 19, 25, 26, 27, 37
mistletoe 24, 25
moisture 9, 18, 36
monkeys 36, 37
monoecious plants 14, 33
mosquitoes 22
mosses **28–29**, 30, 31, 37
moulds 24

nectar 16
needles 32, 34
nests 20, 21
New Zealand 30, 31
North America 20, 32, 33, 34
nutrients 22, 23
nuts 19, 34

oak 34, 35
operculum 28
orchids 15, 17, 19, 36
ovaries 14, 15, 17, 19
overstorey 37
ovules 14, 17
owls 35, 37

oxygen 13, 36
palisade layer 12
parasitic plants **24–25**, 36
pesticides 14
petals 8, 14, 15, 16
petioles 8, 9, 22, 33
photosynthesis 12, 13, 21, 22, 25, 26, 27, 28, 30, 36
photosynthetic pigments 12
phloem 10, 11, 12, 28, 32, 34, 35
pinnae 30
pinnules 30, 31
plumules 18
poison 20, 24
pollen 8, 14, 15, 16, 17, 18, 33, 36
pollination 14, 15, **16–17**, 25, 33
prey 22, 23
prickles 20
prickly pear cactus 20
primary growth 35
primary producers 8
primary roots 34
prothallus stage 31
protonemata stage 28, 29
pumpkins 17

radicles 18
rafflesia 25
rain 15, 20, 21, 35, 36
rainforests 25, **36–37**
receptacles 19
reproduction 14, 27
resins 32
rhizoids 29
rhizomes 30, 31
roots 8, **10–11**, 13, 19, 20, 22, 24, 25, 30, 31, 34, 35, 36
rose hips 19
runner beans 18

sap 9, 11, 12, 13, 32, 34
scales 14, 32, 33
sea 8, 26
sea otters 26
seaweeds 8, **26–27**
secondary growth 35
secondary stems 9, 30
seedlings 10, 17, 18, 19
seeds 13, 16, 17, 18, 19, 24, 28, 32, 33, 34, 36
sepals 9, 14, 15
sex cells 14, 15, 22, 25, 27, 28, 29, 30, 31, 33
shoots 18
shrubs 30, 34, 37
silver fern 30
sloths 36
snakes 36
soil 8, 10, 11, 13, 18, 19, 22, 24, 31, 36, 37
sorus 30
Southeast Asia 25
sperm 27, 28, 29, 31

sphagnum moss 28
spikes 20, 21
spines 21
spongy layer 12
sporangia 30, 31
spore capsules 28, 29
spore-producing stage 28, 31
spores 28, 29, 30, 31
sporophyte stage 28, 31
spring 16, 18, 35
stalks 8, 9, 15, 22, 23, 28, 29
stamens 14, 15, 21
stems 8, 9, **10–11**, 20, 21, 24, 30, 31, 37
stigma 14, 15, 17
stipelets 30
stipes 27, 31
stomata 13, 32
strangler figs 37
strobili 33
styles 14, 15, 17
succulents 21
sugar pine tree 33
sugars 8, 9, 12, 13
summer 16, 35
Sun 8, 9, 10, 13, 19, 21, 22, 24, 25, 26, 36
sundew plant 22

tap roots 11
testas 18
thallus 26, 29
thorns 20, 21
titan arum 15
toxic chemicals 13
trees 8, 10, 24, 25, 29, 34, 35, 36, 37
trigger hairs 22, 23
trunks 10, 32, 34, 35, 37
twigs 24, 32, 33, 35, 37

understorey 37
USA 22, 32

vacuoles 9
vascular bundles 11, 12, 13
vascular plants 30
Venus flytrap 22, 23
vines 25, 36
viscin 24

water 8, 9, 10, 11, 12, 13, 16, 18, 19, 20, 21, 23, 25, 27, 28, 29, 30, 32, 34, 35, 36
water ferns 30
welwitschia plant 9
wind 16, 17, 18, 26, 29, 33, 35
winter 18, 24, 25, 32

xylem 10, 12, 25, 32, 34, 35

yews 32, 33